COLONIZATION FOR KIDS

NORTH AMERICAN EDITION BOOK
EARLY SETTLERS, MIGRATION AND COLONIAL LIFE

3RD GRADE SOCIAL STUDIES

BABY PROFESSOR
EDUCATION KIDS

Speedy Publishing LLC

40 E. Main St. #1156

Newark, DE 19711

www.speedypublishing.com

Copyright 2017

In this book, we're going to talk about colonization in North America. So, let's get right to it!

When the Europeans came to North America, the Native Americans had been living there for thousands of years. The huge numbers of settlers who traveled to North America from the continents of Europe and Africa shaped the early history of the United States. They shaped the events as well as the long-term traditions throughout the nation's history.

Greenland (Denmark)

Baffin Bay

Beaufort Sea

Alaska (US)

Labrador Sea

Gulf of Alaska

Hudson Bay

Canada

Rocky Mountains

United States

PACIFIC

OCEAN

Bahamas

Gulf of Mexico

Cuba

(**Haiti** D

Cayman Is.
(Great Britain)

Jamaica

Mexico

Caribbea

Belize

Guatemala

Honduras

El Salvador

Nicaragua

Panama

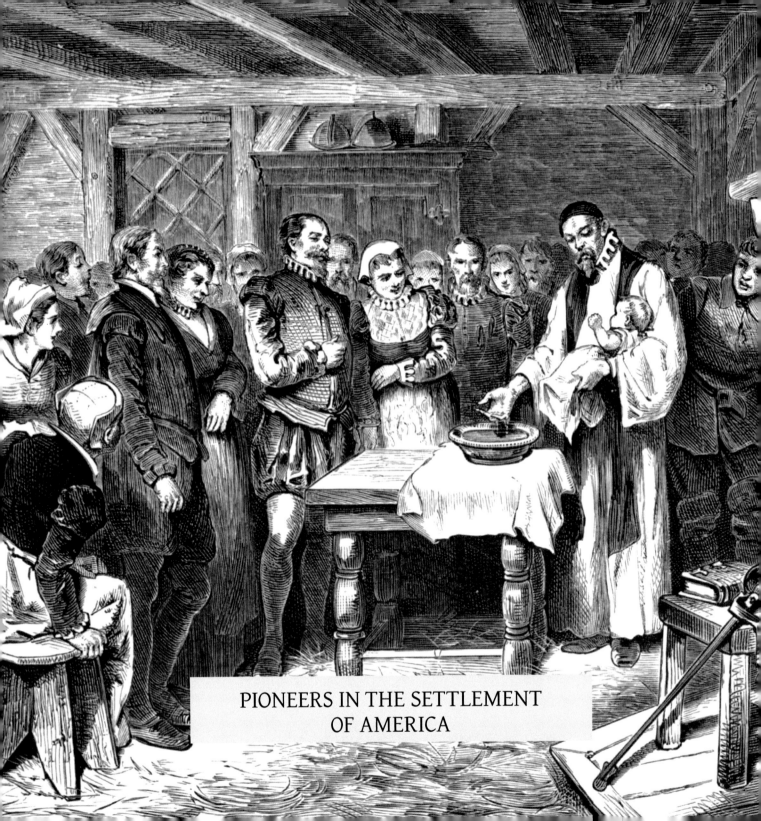

PIONEERS IN THE SETTLEMENT
OF AMERICA

THE HISTORY OF IMMIGRATION FROM 1620 TO 1783

Most of the Europeans that came to the colonies were from Great Britain. However, each group that traveled to North America was a specific group with their own traditions and religious beliefs. They established settlements in different regions of land, separate from each other. Also, there were immigrants from other countries of Europe and slaves that were forced to come from Africa with their owners as well.

THE FIRST ENGLISH SETTLERS COME TO NEW ENGLAND, 1620 TO 1642

The first settlement by English immigrants that became permanent was Jamestown, which was founded in the year 1607 in Virginia. However, larger numbers of immigrants didn't begin coming to North America until 1620. That was the year that the Plymouth Bay Colony, located in Massachusetts, was established by the religious settlers we know today as the Pilgrims.

The Church of England was the official church. The Pilgrims wanted to worship in a different way so they broke with the Church of England and, because of this, they were described as Separatists.

RELIGIOUS SETTLERS OF PLYMOUTH

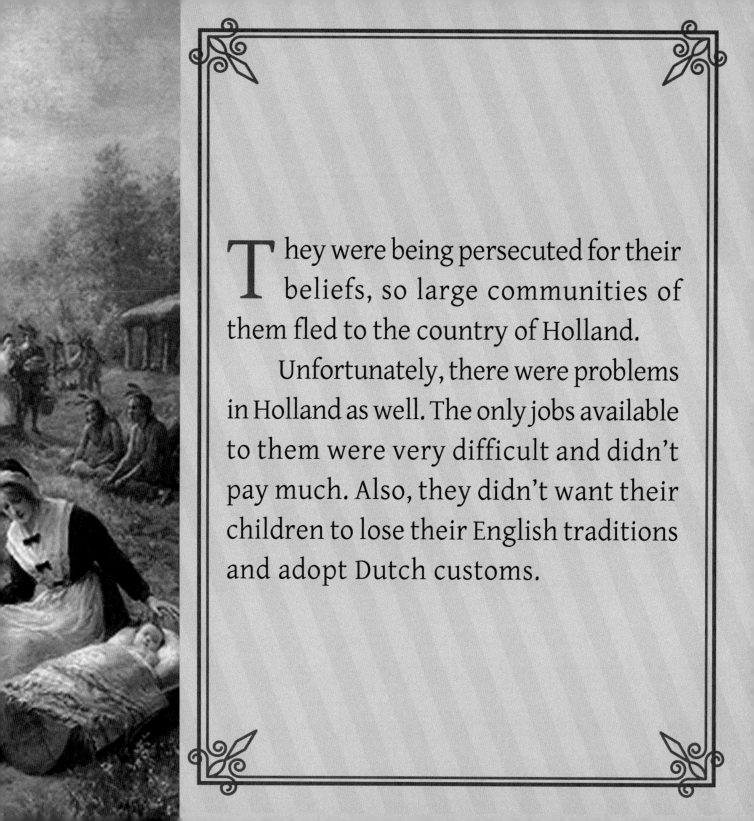

They were being persecuted for their beliefs, so large communities of them fled to the country of Holland.

Unfortunately, there were problems in Holland as well. The only jobs available to them were very difficult and didn't pay much. Also, they didn't want their children to lose their English traditions and adopt Dutch customs.

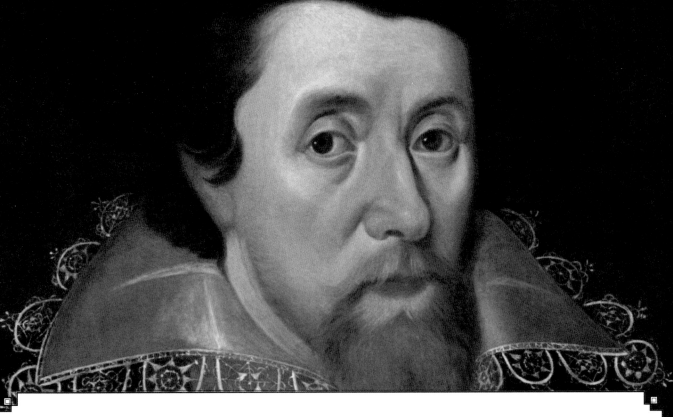

The leaders of their group persuaded King James I, England's king, to give them permission to travel and settle in America.

The London Virginia Company agreed to finance their voyage. In return, the settlers were obligated to give the proceeds of the crops they planned to farm once they got to the New World.

The Mayflower, 1620, Plymouth, Mass.

THE MAYFLOWER, 1620

In mid-September of the year 1620, a ship called the Mayflower sailed from the port of Plymouth in England. On board were 102 passengers and 41 of them were Pilgrims. It took eight weeks before they landed at Cape Cod in the region that is known as modern-day Massachusetts. However, in that location, their encounters with the Native Americans were bordering on violent so they decided to move on to Plymouth Bay by the end of the year.

T hey had a very difficult time that first winter as they also did with subsequent winters. Eventually, with persistence, and with new arrivals, this colony became one of the core centers of population in America.

A MAP OF NEW AMSTERDAM IN 1660, MANHATTAN

A decade later, another religious group came to America. They wanted to worship in the established Church of England, but they believed that it needed to go through a purification process. They were called Puritans. Seventeen ships with Puritan passengers set sail for America in 1630.

JOHN WINTHROP

T heir leader, who was named John Winthrop, sailed on the ship that was named the Arabella. They left England at a time when there were tensions between the Puritans and the established church. William Laud, who was the Church of England's archbishop wanted to eliminate their influence from the church.

At the same time King Charles I had taken power over the country without consulting Parliament. These events led to a civil war in England that lasted nine years. It was a time when the economy was in trouble and the Puritans were not welcome in England.

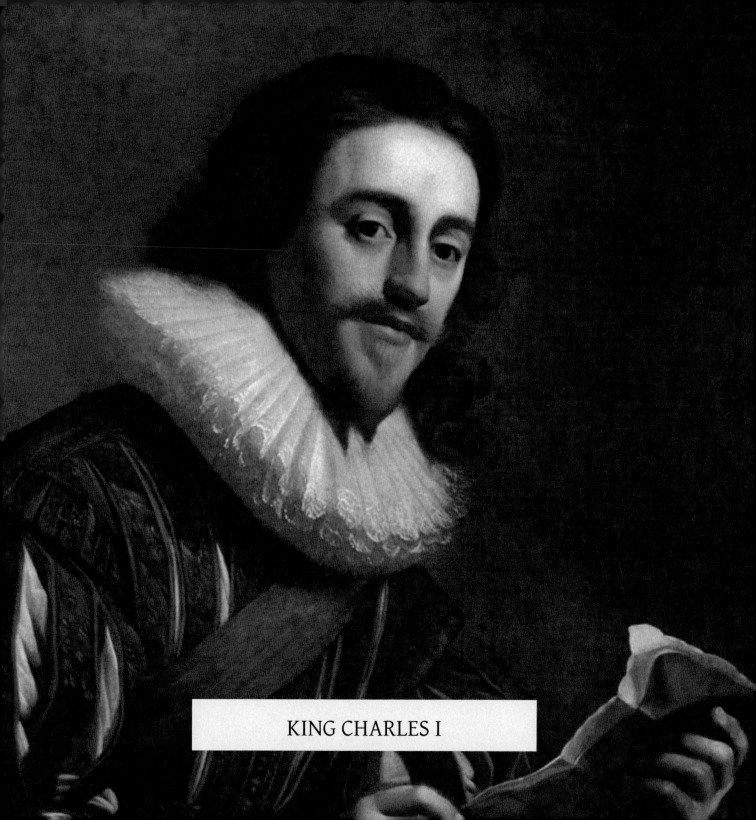

KING CHARLES I

THE GREAT MIGRATION

During the years 1630 to 1640, a great migration occurred. About 200 ships arrived during this decade with another 20,000 people who arrived to settle in the New World. This huge population was mostly Puritans escaping England.

They settled north of Plymouth Bay. This region was described as the Massachusetts Bay Colony.

The colony had major centers along the east coast of what is now Massachusetts with concentrated population in the city of Boston and the city of Salem.

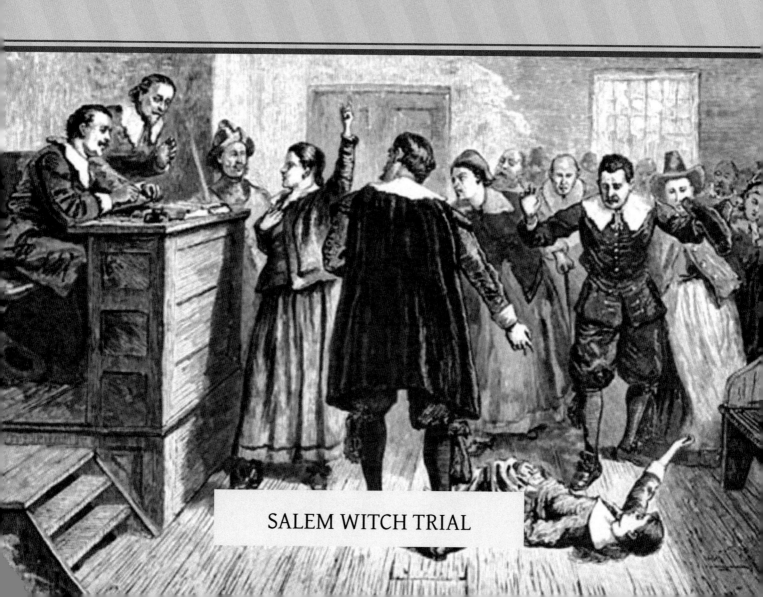

SALEM WITCH TRIAL

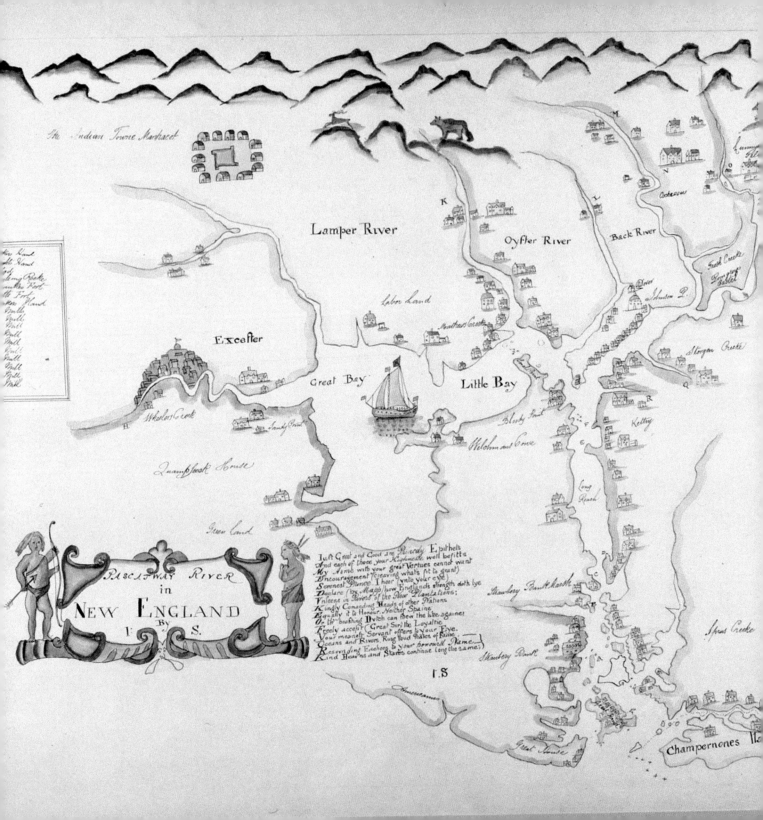

The Indian Towne Machacot

Lamper River

Oyfter River

Back River

K

M

N

O

Cocheco

Freſh Creeke

Labor Land

Exeſter

Matheus Creeke

Johnson P.

Morgan Creeke

Q

Great Bay

Little Bay

Bloody Point

R

Kettry

Wheelers Creeke

Sandy Point

Welchmans Cove

Quampſeak Houſe

Long Reach

Green Land

PASCATWAY RIVER
in
NEW ENGLAND
BY
I S

Juſt Great and Good and Pincely Epithets
And each of theſe your Highneſſe well befitts
My Aime with your great Vertues cannot want
Encouragement (cleaving vnto your eye
Sereneſt Prince I hear (vnto your eye
Declare (by Mapp) how Englands ſtrength doth lye
Vnſeene in ſeveral of the New Plantations;
Kingly Comanding Heads of other Nations
Equally it to Honour. Neither Spaine
Or th' boaſting Dutch can ſhew the like againe:
Freely accept (Great Sir) the Loyaltie
Your meaneſt Servant offers to your Eye.
Oceans and Rivers Ring loud ſtates of Fame
Reſerveing Echoes to your farewell Name;
Kind Heav'ns and States continue long the ſame:

I S

Stawbery Banck marſh

Spras Creeke

Stawbery Bank

A

B

C

D

Great Houſe

Champernones Ila

This was the largest group of people who had ever arrived during a brief span of time and after this, the pace of migration slowed. However, the population continued to grow and the descendants of these original settlers spread out throughout New England and eventually began to travel to the west.

ENGLISH SETTLEMENT IN VIRGINIA FROM 1642 TO 1675

South of the Massachusetts Bay Colony, the early settlements in Virginia had barely been able to survive. However, as the population stopped coming in droves to Massachusetts, the population of Virginia began to grow. In the year 1642, only about 8,000 settlers were established in Virginia. At that time, Sir William Berkeley was elected governor of the colony. He would remain governor for over 30 years.

He decided that he wanted some of England's most important members of society to come to Virginia.

SIR WILLIAM BERKELEY

At that point, the tide had turned in England in regard to the Puritans. They had risen to power and King Charles I had been executed in the year 1649.

Many of America's future leaders came from the elite group of people who were wealthy aristocrats in England and came to America to live. However, not all the settlers were from this upper level of society.

About 75% of the new settlers who came to Virginia through the late 17th century were servants. They were called "indentured" because they were bound to serve their masters without any wages and in return they were given the opportunity to come to the new country. Because of this, the society in Virginia was very unequal for a long time.

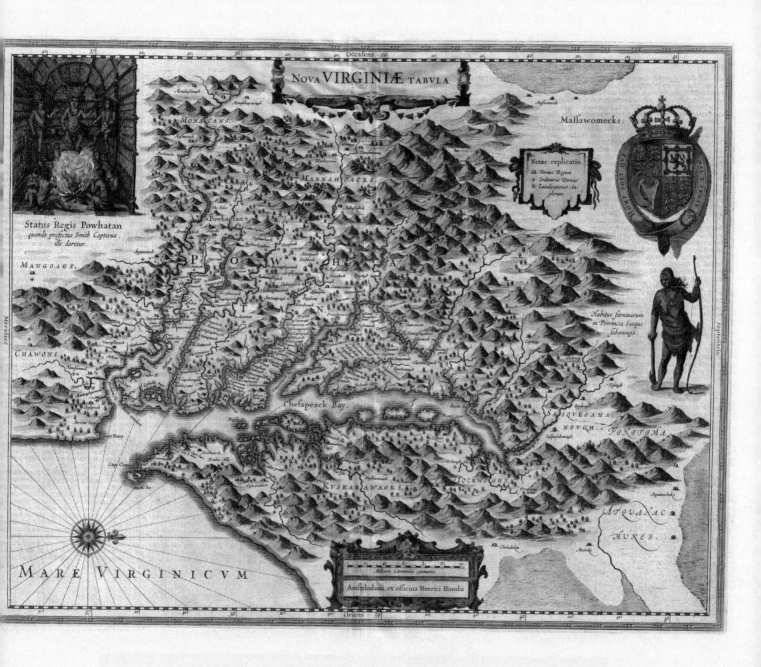

MAP OF VIGINIA 1630

By the year 1660, the population there was about 30,000 settlers. The region that eventually became the state of Maryland had a large population of servants as well, at least 4,000 around the year 1660.

THE IMMIGRATION OF
QUAKERS FROM 1675 TO 1725

Another religious group began coming to America in large numbers around 1675. These Christians were called the Quakers and they believed very strongly in equality for all and an inwardly directed view of faith. The Quakers disliked social levels so they were sometimes persecuted in their native land of England.

Very soon after they established their religious beliefs, they began to come to America.

CROSSING DELAWARE RIVER

They first came to West Jersey in the region of Salem. Subsequent ships arrived in Delaware Bay.

The Quakers came in such large numbers that they would be ranked as the third most populated religion in the colonies by the year 1750. The leader of the Quakers was a man by the name of William Penn. His dream was to create a region dedicated to Quakers in New England. He wanted to encourage Quakers from England to come there.

WILLIAM PENN

In the year 1681, he received a charter for 45,000 square miles of land. The charter was given to him by King Charles II and the king is the one who named the region Pennsylvania after William Penn.

SOUTH RENOVO, PENNSYLVANIA
HOUSES TODAY

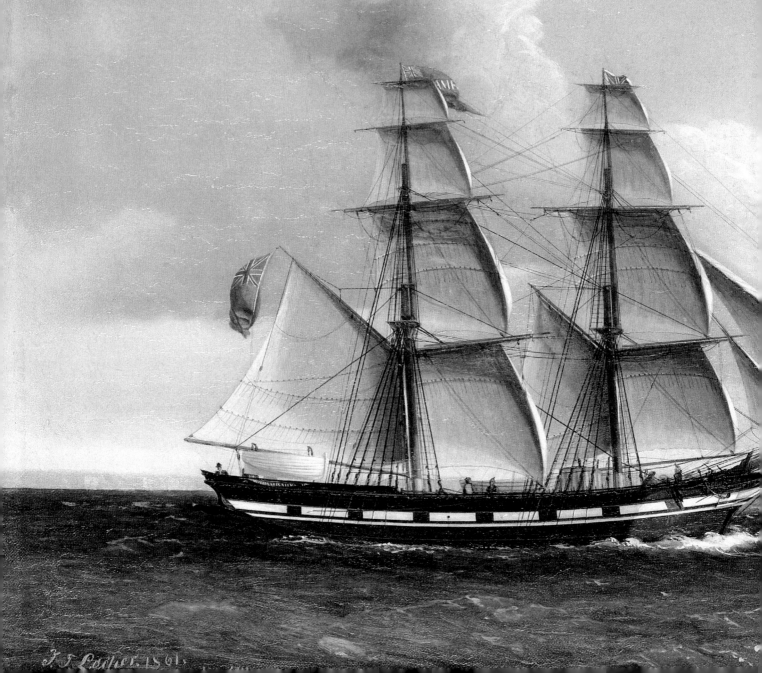

The following year, Penn arrived there on a ship that was called "Welcome."

Penn was a firm believer in tolerance of all religions so many other groups came to Pennsylvania in addition to the Quakers.

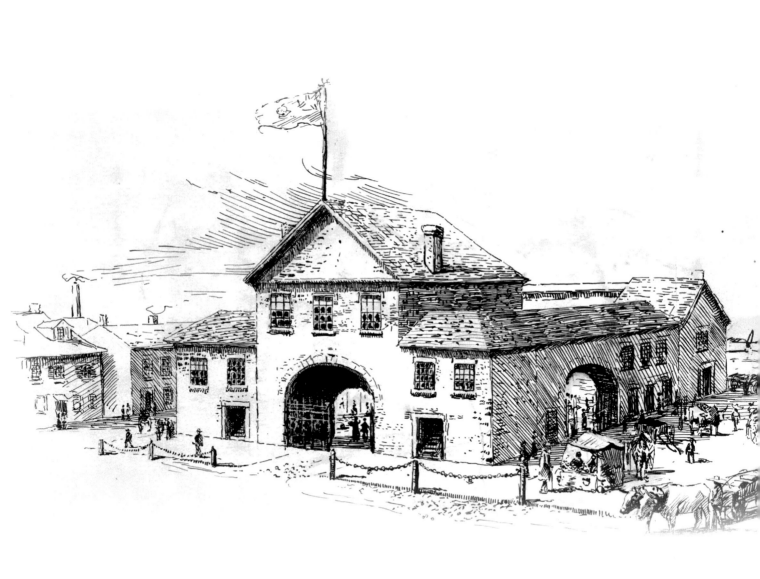

THE SCOTTISH, SCOTCH IRISH, & ENGLISH IMMIGRATION FROM 1715 TO 1775

Most of the people from Irish descent who came to America prior to the 19th century were of Scotch-Irish descent. People who migrated to the western edges of the colonies were mostly from the northern region of England, the country of Scotland, and Scottish-Irish people from Northern Ireland.

Some of these waves of immigrants came because of famines due to the failures of crops. The lands along the east coast were already quite populated at this time.

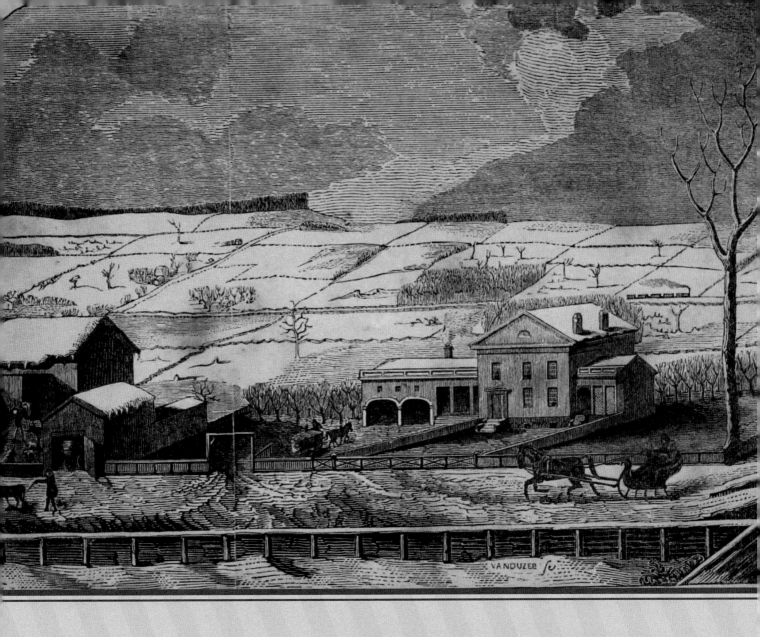

These hardy people and their descendants became the pioneers as the western expansion began.

THE NORWEGIANS DISCOVERED CANADA

DUTCH, SWEDISH AND GERMAN IMMIGRATION FROM 1630 TO 1783

From 1630 through 1783, there was a large group of immigrants that came to America from the European countries of Holland, Sweden, and Germany. As with the other settlers, these individuals were experiencing hardship or political chaos and they saw the New World as an opportunity to change their lives.

SLAVES FROM AFRICA FROM 1640 TO 1783

Some people didn't want to come to America but they were forced to come. When the first Census was taken in 1790, people from Africa who had been brought to America as slaves made up 20% of the population.

SUMMARY

There were Native Americans living in the region where the British outposts were established in the New World. Beginning around 1607, settlers who were born in England came to the regions that we now know as Massachusetts and Virginia. It took several decades for these settlements to become established.

The English settlers were primarily driven by the need to be able to worship their own way. They didn't agree with the rules and traditions of the established Church of England.

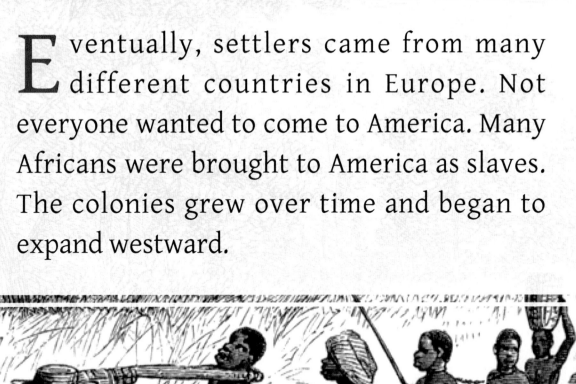

Eventually, settlers came from many different countries in Europe. Not everyone wanted to come to America. Many Africans were brought to America as slaves. The colonies grew over time and began to expand westward.

Awesome! Now that you've read about colonization in North America, you may want to read about why the colonies broke away from Great Britain in the Baby Professor book Explaining the Stamp and Townshend Acts.

Made in the USA
Coppell, TX
21 October 2020